I0756305

FINISHING LINE PRESS
www.finishinglinepress.com

the light can be something you love all on your own

poems by

stephanie e. glass

Finishing Line Press
Georgetown, Kentucky

the light can be something you love all on your own

this book is dedicated to anyone who needs to be reminded:
you are made of metal and magic
&
in celebration of Andrea Gibson
who taught me a kinder way to say my own name

ISBN 979-8-89990-474-5 First Edition

ACKNOWLEDGMENTS

"letter to my friend after swimming" was first published in the December 2024 edition of *Rattle Poetry Magazine.*

"you're so fucking gay" was first published in The Quarter(ly) Journal in the 2025 edition titled *This is Where We are Now.*

"shuffling the deck" was first published by *Writers in the Attic*, in the 2025 anthology.

All my gratitude to Timothy Green and the team at *Rattle Poetry Magazine*, and to Chris Smith, editor of the *Quarter(ly) Journal* who were the origional publishers of these poems, with some slight alterations.

Whitney Tewahade was instrumental in her design of the cover of this text. I will forever appreciate the love of Toadstool Park that we share, and her desire to honor the imagined cover I held in my mind as something precious. I consider it an honor to weave our art together through this collection.

Publisher: Leah Huete de Maines
Editor: Christen Kincaid
Cover Art: Whitney Tewahade
Author Photo: Treasa Hunt
Cover Design: Elizabeth Maines McCleavy

Order online: www.finishinglinepress.com
also available on amazon.com

Author inquiries and mail orders:
Finishing Line Press
PO Box 1626
Georgetown, Kentucky 40324
USA

Contents

mom, you wore the dress to the playground 1

you took my teeth 3

october is a silent month 5

there was good weather on your birthday this year 6

this is the process of driving: 7

here the falling skylarks 8

death at white river creek 9

through winter 11

forgive me 12

point blank and nameless 13

shuffling the deck 14

chokecherries and idioms 16

i walk beneath 18

the light can be something that you love all on your own 19

a decomposition 20

you're so fucking gay 21

on the streets of lincoln, nebraska 23

a letter to my friend after swimming 24

the soup 25

petal-skirts 27

we do something normal 28

some of this space 30

here 32

table setting 34

mom, you wore the dress to the playground

the one with small yellow flowers.   perspective is everything.
looking up at you then
my small hands around the metal chain of a swing set   i thought
that they were real.

i thought that you were blooming where you stood.
mom, do you remember   how i would go out at twilight   the
night too humid for sleep   & walk in loops around the
neighborhood?

did you even know i was not in my bed? i came home with mosquito
bites dotting my arms   fire ant bites on my feet.   sleeping
until afternoon took over   the house

because why do girls need school   once we know enough to
cook for our husbands?

i remember you convinced a cop once   that you were swerving
through traffic   because you were eating skittles. i remember
those skittles: the bright red bag & your

fingers painted pink with food coloring and saliva. you were tasting
the rainbow.

those skittles: stored in your purse   next to an orange bottle of
oxy.   amelia used to steal them from your bag. my little
sister.   two years younger than me.   me: the
protector   who failed.

i'm still waiting   for the paperwork to come in
but sometimes I think autism saved my life.

it's hard to go off track   when you have to follow the rules
if you want to be able to breathe.

sorry   i couldn't follow your rules, mom.   not sorry for
breathing. not sorry for not taking those pills

on that RV park bathroom floor.

you told me to *do it*   *if you're going to do it*   *but—for god's*
sake—stop   *being a little bitch and wasting my time.*

i digress   i was remembering: the officer.   the skittles.
the car   that almost crashed.

framed   in the window   of the old white van: amelia's arm,
a railroad track of thick pink scars   on tan skin. She was always
tugging her sleeves   down.

we were always pretending   the scars did not exist.

i remember   i always remember: she used to take deep
breaths   one right after the other and let the neighborhood
boy   put his hands over her heart &   press
until she fainted.

lying there on the ground.   i think perhaps   she just
didn't want to feel it anymore.   perhaps she just wanted
to rest.

walking through a different town   in a different state   in
a different century   i find a dead coyote
lying in a neighbor's yard.   i don't worry
as i dial the police.   i just dial.   they didn't

save us then &   there's nothing to save now.   we saved ourselves
or we didn't.

the coyote's fur   so soft & yellow.
i think of my mother's dress.
the flowers: a print

on fabric.

you took my teeth

it's a joke of the highest order—
the way you pull my teeth from my jaw.

my mouth is filling with blood
words dribbling down

my lips. red slime and gaping
sockets. take your fingers off

my flailing tongue.
i caught your crimes on

camera. saved on the cloud. the way we do things now.
everything safe. everything preserved.

we are over but the record still exists.
the bruises faded but my mind still scarred.

your voice still there,
haunting my phone with the ghost of words i once tolerated.

hit play, hear
myself laughing as i try to lighten the mood.

remember thinking: make it a joke, make it
a punchline, and i do, but it lands on my jaw.

swear babe, no more games for 6 months. just so we can get back on our feet.
haha, lol. ROTFL. a tooth hits the floor.

i say: *i,* ██████████, *swear i won't buy any more games for 6 months.*
you repeat with revisions: *i,* ██████████, *swear i will kill my wife.*

i am laughing on record.
my laughter: sharp as an incisor.

you say it again for emphasis.
you swear it: *i,* ████████, *swear that will kill my wife.*
on the other end of the recording: i can hear the clatter—

your fingers on a gaming controller. you never stop playing.

in the present, listening to the past, it plays out:
the future

that would have been
if i had stayed.

even as i run my tongue over my steady teeth, i hear it:
the impact of fist on bone, my teeth

hitting the ground.
the echo of my own laughter

rings in my ears and
the taste of the blood not spilled haunts my tongue

i open the iPhone, play it for a friend, then play it for my therapist,
to see if they can taste it too.

there it is, that line: *i swear i will kill my wife.*
gigabytes of my terrified laughter on repeat.

a joke of the highest order.

october is a silent month

after the divorce / jack-o-lanterns appear / and age / day by day
their carved teeth / curl / into witches gums.
i pick up / the dropped stitches
of my life / and continued to knit / myself into forward motion.

every morning / through this silence / i walk my son to the
school and leave him / at the door.

every morning i ask myself / have i left something behind?
in all the wanting of this life / have i abandoned another self
/ another possibility / another pathway that would have lead to
something
greater.

at the end of the day / milo looks up at me / with ears big enough to
catch wind / cheeks defined by freckles / he asks how frost coats
the body of a leaf / how snow forms and falls
and accumulates / and i know

that i am / the only self
i could ever be.

there was good weather on your birthday this year

but you can't feel it / your skin thickened with age / and thoughts of
another day / another time:

the density of the strawberry cheesecake / your mother made you for
your sixteenth birthday / the fist your father sent through it / when
you asked him to come to the table / to sing /
the way he called you a fat little bitch / said he'd done you a favor.

after the storm passed / your mother /
picked you up off the floor

and knelt at your feet / cleaned / the swirls of pink and white off your
shoes / you couldn't see her face as she asked

why you had to go and run / your mouth and make him do it.

yesterday / the cottonwood trees were turning yellow / and the air
smelled like water and you were not alone / but with someone who
was only kind to you

but despite that goodness / today is your birthday / and every
birthday you turn 16 again /
and see your mother's body

bent over a dirty floor / you know that every birthday you will be / 30
again and she will be fresh / dead / wrong or right

you will not say goodbye / or any words at all / so today it is dry
despite the rain /
and standing in the liminal space of your own age

you cannot perceive the beauty / or the loss
of it all.

this is the process of driving:

turn the key / engage the gears / release the brake
countless drives / on my own / down the same strip of road
to grab a burger at the local dive / or a hike in the wilderness
positioned just outside the contained / order of population.

the process is different today / my son in the backseat
offering a screaming commentary / and you riding shotgun

always the musical connoisseur / this summer deprived of options
hungry for music / the way i am hungry for time / with you

you change the track / and sia is singing *chandelier* over
the crackle of my blown out speakers

this simple task / driving from home / to place
to home again / the time it takes / not a burden

but a joy / in which i find
myself smiling / to share
such an ordinary / happiness.

here the falling skylarks

find the may pole where the log branch hums / where do you look for the functional blue? / skylarks fall / from the air / like blankets

atop blankets / cold toes like grapes or grape / scented bubbles pop / from their hides to sit on the miraculous vine / twine around the bushes and beavers /

link cold thoughts to hot / toddies in crone hands / don't say safe here / here is everywhere and / everywhere /

never existed / present days / present you with / armor and shield / accept the mountain and the valley / take water into your bone marrow and

make yourself into broth / infuse the sky with the saliva / that sits at the bottom / of your mouth

and sip at the blue / with the functional blue / of your own sweet lips.

death at white river creek

mom, i killed you a fish today.
you are too far gone to eat with us.
but still, for you,
i killed the fish.

the car smelled of lake the whole drive home.
every so often
the bluegill flipped
around on the paper where i set it. proving what
i am already aware of:
i don't quite know what i'm doing yet.

my kitchen was warm and bright. i sharpened
the knife.
my son and i watched
a youtube video on how to clean
something dead and turn it into life. butter melted in the pan.
my knife scraped away scales
and severed the spinal cord. thunk.
the guts will make it to my garden.
a place you never got to see.

it had eaten my fly, back there
on the dock at white river creek, the pointed barb wrapped up
in gills and flesh.
i could not pry it free and would not have saved him if i had.
blood already seeping through
gills to tint my hands with a sunset of red.
death is kinder and consumption is gratitude.

mom, can we learn after we die?
mom, can i teach you how to catch a fish?
mom, can i teach you how to kill without malice,
to love without fists,
to eat the buttery remains with your child

on the floor—

a picnic of gratitude.

sit with me, eat, and watch
the light on the water.

through winter

i text him a poem by raymond
carver / the one about the rain / he says
he likes the idiom at the end and
for a moment / we talk / about words
instead of snow.

the spring is creeping / up and i've
started buying dirt to fill
my garden bed / and seeds
are sprouting / in my window / and
little green buds of newly formed herbs / poke

through the dirt / i want to tell him all these things

but i do not / i save them for later

because / if given half a chance
i hope to see him / again

if only / to talk / about the heat
and my longing / for rain.

forgive me

she is named june / the little girl / her hair a white-blond tangle / her eyes studious / as she looks ahead / to where milo runs / through the sun-drunk plains / she is not born / and i know now / never will be / and if you had loved me / and wanted to create this / picture of a life together / this little girl named june / she would not have been the girl i am writing now / the way you are not / the way i write you / standing behind me / in the red flannel shirt / which buttons so neatly at the wrists

i have chosen it for you / the way i choose everything in the world / that lives / in the pink light / behind my closed eyes / our daughter's fine blond hair / her eyes / blue / like yours /

look at me / at how i keep adding detail: that we're half a mile down a dirt road / from a little yellow farmhouse in kansas / where i bake bread and pull bindweed from the garden / and you maintain the fenceline / i blink:

the weight of our daughter rests casually on my hip / the space between my back and your chest / cut down / to barely an
inch.

or milo's smile / his long leggy stride / half him / half who i hope he'll be / his arms spread wide enough to / hold onto the whole earth.

point blank and nameless

when i / run from a name / it is always my father's / except when it is my own / *johnny* / my mother said / begged / pled /   her body: a field of rubble /   standing inside a door frame / i saw the white flem / crusted in the corners of her mouth / smelled the piss and shit / lingering in the air / but it is the gnarled bones of her hands / that hold me / still / claws to catch him / grasp his fist / caress his face / tenderly run her swollen knuckles / over the rhinophyma that marred his skin / hers was a love so hungry / it devoured the sky / so precious / it was worth dying for

she longed / only to pull a weapon closer to her / his words / the muzzle of a beloved gun / pressed against her skull / she wanted to hold the violence of his hands in her own / mangled / fingers / that day / i was ten years old / and seven / and six / and three /
two /
one.

that day / in that doorway / i was still bright with fading sunlight / my spine still remembering the pressure of my favorite / reading tree /

the light /

almost /

remained.

but her voice / her unending torrents of grief / like vomit dribbling over the edge of a table / leaves me paralyzed / stuck / in the place between inside / and out / *johnyjohnyjohny* / a tattoo / on my memories / please / take it away. /   her face / her face / my god / her hands

but how can i blame her? / later i will say the names of men / in that same tone / and i will break myself over an altar / as if to exorcize my mother's voice from my throat /

to empty my hands / of her broken / delicate / bones.

shuffling the deck

as i shuffle tarot cards / shadows of a black cat / run over my shoes / sitting on your rusty tailgate / i pull the world[1] from the deck / and set the world aside to / watch water droplets / glimmering / like sequins on your denim jeans

some nights watching the sequins / shine is all i have / others i don't have even that.

i start to talk about god / in your mother's house / and watch your face shut / watch your eyes lock / feel my throat close around / what i do not say / i want to hold up a mirror / and show you your father's face / but i do not want to add to your pain / so i let you add to mine.

sitting at your mother's table / i do not know what you need / and you will not tell me. / i read / your face: *if you were what i wanted / you would know / without a word. i almost want / to say / that's not how this works / love is understanding and / understanding is work.* / but i've said it before and / i'm tired / of pretending / that this is love.

but when we talk about god / or rather the absence of god / alone in your inherited truck / me pulling the hanged man[2] and shuffling the deck / in your barely-used passenger seat / you in the broken-down driver seat / a pillow shoved under one asscheek / to save your broken back /
there /
there /
we're on point.

there / railroad earth / sings about being in tune.

through a spiderwebbed wind / shield I see sleeping nests / of yesterday's birds awaken / and / flame across the sky / i burn the living / and burn your memory / but we flare up like a tickle / in the back of my throat / god / we're all on fire with something / aren't we?

like a show on my iris / your games of hide and seek play out / i watch you move / northbound / then west / but you always stop at the wall of your fear.

the postcard on your mother's fridge contains / a poem and your name you love / her and so you / write to her / i love you and so i write to you / you write back once / but not more / i always / want more / you do not have that to give / at least not to me

watch me stand witness like a widow: / i am holding out my empty hands / understand this / they deserve
to be filled

i slip off the tailgate and shuffle / the deck / i pull the world / and press it to my chest / with both hands

---

1 end of a life cycle / beginning a new one
2 sacrifice / surrender / suspension in time

chokecherries and idioms

halfway inside a bush / i admire / the striations
marking the golden berries.

though some are beak-plucked / and leaking juice / others are fat
and lovely in / their roundness / you combine idioms / say that
we're cherry-picking low-hanging fruit / then dream of being a
bear / the sun sings out

offering her full voice / and i relish
the sensation of / sweat seeping
through the fabric of my shirt

branches prickle / against my arm /
i am / in this moment / defined / by the weight
of my full hands.

later
you will move / around my kitchen
with your own personal brand / of rapidity

for you / this moment is already over / but the movie / plays on
the camera shifts / shows

my eyes / often / on your back / watching
the wingspan of your shoulder blades

shifting as you strain / warm chokecherries
through cheesecloth / stir together the
juice, sugar, pectin, and citrus

i will remember how to do this later / i will pick sandhill plums
on my own / make jelly / on my own / i will leave because i have to /
because almost enough / is still not / enough

but you are not gone yet / here in my kitchen / in this preserved
moment / you set your body to a staccato rhythm
one i have studied / for it is a gift to understand / someone who is

so nearly a language of their own
each separate beat of movement coming together / to form
something whole

something comforting / and just as warm / as the scent
of my kitchen / the muted sunlight / drifting through the glass of my
window.

i will miss the language / of your hands / when they are gone / from
my life.

i walk beneath

can the sky be measured in / depth?

i'd like to think so / we walked this earth of ours together once

it was ours / once /

hours spent / as if they counted / heads tipped back / admiring the sky

we never lied / we were always / here.

you have thought of me since / i do not doubt this / but together is just a word / unless we / reach for each other.

time is enough / to break us / i am not confused / if we do not walk / toward each other / we make a choice.

you have made a choice / you and your large hands / your soft voice / your long legs / that could walk the plains so much faster than mine / you have chosen to drift / far / from me / as if i were not / valuable / as if i did not deserve to be hungered for / when i think of the future / you have shifted out of sight / this door

is closed / for my comfort / i do not dream / it open / instead i just / leave / and what was complicated / unravels / what was chained / is unchained / there is no tape to rewind /

i spacewalk into my / life /

and release you. we are / a scarf unraveled / your memory: a single strand of / yarn.

slim and soft / floating away from me / i am /

untethered

free

to walk beneath the stars / with no memory of stars

i do not need your eyes / i can see that / they are as beautiful / as all of creation.

the light can be something that you love all on your own

do you remember sitting with me / beneath an eruption of stars? / two camp chairs next to each other / and empty promises on our lips / i'd hiked out to your camp / my tent in my pack / i was trying so hard to be the kind of person / you could love

our dinner: sauteed morels / that you'd picked with your father dipped in / an under-seasoned mixture / of eggs, salt / and flour / fried in butter / i made a feast of them / as if this gesture / was evidence / of something more / than your hunger / i built my hope / here / on mushrooms / and picking sandhill plums / and talking about the beauty of / the blue light on the plains / the passing moments / where you found me worthy of your time

if i could go back / i'd tell myself: / the light can be something you love / all on your own / i'd tell myself: / darling, go make yourself a feast / and share it with someone who wants you / who comes to you hungry for you / just as you are / hunger for yourself / just as you are / do not accept the table leavings / do not accept a place in the corner of his life / you are too wild and extraordinary / to be set aside so easily / too generous / to grieve / the absence / of someone who didn't notice you / were leaving / until you were already gone.

a decomposition

my cat has killed / another bird / and left its body / for me / to find
beneath / the clothesline / cleanly dead / a broken neck perhaps

though dead

the feathers / are not yet / brittle / though dead / the body still
plump / as if this bird is not yet aware / of its own demise.

but give it a week.

each day / as i walk the space / from my back door

to my small garden / i bear witness as / the facsimile of life oozes into
the grass / leaving bones / beak / frangible feathers / and little else /
behind.

you're so fucking gay

and what if I'm not gay enough? / i don't fuck on the first/second/third date / except for when i do / and / i mean / i'm not a virgin / but / i feel like one here / in your bed / on the tenth date / with the sheets sprawled around us / and your arm around my shoulder / your fingers sneaking beneath the spaghetti strap on my shoulder / tracing circles under the skin / raising goose bumps / and this is all the wanting in the world / pressing me into the mattress / in a way / i don't know how to act on / because i've fucked / but i haven't fucked a girl yet / more importantly / i haven't fucked you yet. / because fuck / the gender constructs and the performativity / its the you of it all that matters. / it's the me of it all that matters.

damn it

am i getting it right? / saying it right? / fuck the bravado: i'm gay enough to want you / gay enough to imagine coming home to you / gay enough to want to clean our home together / gay enough to wake from dreams where i am touching you / pressing my palm flat against your stomach / running my tongue across your shoulder blade. i want to be sitting / cross legged on the floor / reorganizing the fridge while you do the dishes.

i want to come / home to you   i'm gay enough to write this poem

but am i gay enough that these words will stick the landing? / i don't want to fuck unless i'm so caught up in the person / in their words / their heart / their mind / their body / that i can feel it in my marrow: i need to touch / taste / inhale them… / so i waited until it mattered. / i want you to know that /
you matter.

we're lying in bed / and i want to kiss you / but i also want to tell you a story:

the first girl i touched / my hand in her hand or her hand in mine both of us 16 / captured on video at mormon church camp / her / looking straight up like avril lavigne in that sk8ter boi music video / i

watched on repeat / her: poking me to make me laugh, laughing at
my laugh / me, smiling, green haired and pink cheeked / i was young
enough to know / how i felt / ~~without the words to say it~~ / with the
knowledge that it wasn't safe to say it / that if i said it i wouldn't have
permission to exist / sixteen years old / with hellfire burning in my
parents' mouths / the memory of a friend / sent to a conversion camp
/ never heard from again / i knew i was myself / anyway / indelible
/ immutable / i'm gay enough / that just is / the way i think you're
handsomeandbeautifulandjesusmotherfuckingchrist sexy as hell
when you smile / here's facts: that just is. / i just am. / we just /
          are.
i / am / gay / enough. / to be here in this bed / with you / reaching
out / to touch your cheek / with my hand / language disappears / in
some kind of beautiful ordinary / no one can touch us / here is the
only place left / the light from the television flickers / dims / and /
together / we /

                                                  exist.

on the streets of lincoln, nebraska

a woman kneels, her body folded into a sort of child's pose.

light shines through / the gap / between her heel and her sandal

all of her weight / pressing / into her toes / the nails sparkle / a bright candy apple red.

her cheek kisses the side / walk's rough surface / as she murmurs softly to the ground / or perhaps her phone / though I cannot see it / or perhaps she has lost an earring

or her mind / i prefer to imagine / that she is talking / to god or the earth / an act i too often abstain from for fear / of losing myself on my knees / to something i cannot / should not /

understand.

a letter to my friend after swimming

to alyssa

hey girl / so i keep taking milo to the pool / he's on the swim team now / level one/ he's still learning to blow bubbles and float and breathe / while he swims i swim / freestyle and breaststroke and butterfly / and / i'm learning to breathe too / learning to breathe seems like it should be easy / but it's like / like learning to walk like learning to blink / like learning to look at someone and know that you love them / like learning to pick up the pieces / after that person disappears / i always pick up the pieces / get my son to the pool on time / the dentist on time / the doctor on time / school on time / i am on time / i'm learning how to breathe / and every breath is ten thoughts right now / Isn't that just how it works sometimes? sometimes a breath is just a breath and / sometimes it's everything you can do to inhale without drowning / but at the end of my swim he comes through the double doors toward me / running the way you run when you can't run by the pool / to stand over me / where i'm waiting after finishing my lap / and my watch is counting down to the next repetition / the next series of strokes through the sterile blue the next exhalation of everything i've got into bubbles and motion and i'm inhaling the scent of chlorine like it's peace / and there he is smiling like he's won the lottery because it's the end of the lesson and he / gets to swim / with his mom / and girl, i gotta tell you / in that moment / i don't have to think / about breathing.

the soup

we're all happening at once
the falling in love
the falling out of it
identities shifting

mercury in a vile
linguistic observations and absolutions
at the end of the world
we don't know how to stop the all-at-once

on my therapist's couch
i call it a soup

like any writer worth her salt
at first i try to revise

pull the ingredients out one by one
examine them
a grammar check
a proof read
a line-by-line dissection that stops the thing i love
from being the thing i love

all this analysis when we're all just trying
to stay out of the path of the landslide
and then when it inevitably takes us
we're left just trying to keep our feet
to keep our cool

don't you know we're all uncool
at the end of the world?
don't you know we're all exceeding
our capacity for fuck yous and failures
and they've hidden the fuel gauge
so that we can't see that the tank on the rescue vehicle
is below empty?

we can't see that we're all underwater together
the teleprompter told us that light does not exist
and so by silent consensus we've all stopped looking for it
we pull away from every touch
every honest word is too much

we burn out our energy in the act of evasion
all the while our souls are crying *lonely*
the way a person stranded in the desert
might cry *water*.

petal skirts

after talking with ann krejci in the garden

let's watch the poppies
spit their
orange petals
to the ground.
in earlier days of summer
they were all dressed up and
had no opinion about having
somewhere to go.

let's sit a while
in the sweet sunlight
and think about how simple it is
to stay
in just one place.

let us be rooted here
our bare feet on the earth,
our palms against grass.

there's an ache in my left sole
from where i pulled the goathead
from my barely calloused skin.
i have always been penetrable.

sitting here in observation
of the world, with you,
then without you, still i know:
that all is part of all the rest.

we do something normal

after attending the black hills community theatre's performance of cabaret

even as we fear / the bells might be tolling for our country / we go to
the theater / where the cast of cabaret take the stage / and yes there
are high kicks / and dancers in feathered costumes / but there's also
grief / and the descent of a country into a future filled / with the
ruthless extermination of a people / of *people*
sitting there in that theater seat / i sip moscato as you sip your beer /
i realize how foolish i was to think that this would be some romp / set
within a tragedy /
i am grateful for your hand / brushing against my shoulder / pulling
me back into my body / the play
ends
without fanfare / there is no resolution /
to the holocaust that is coming / no elegant bowing and curtseying /
no one holds flowers / no one beams / they stare us down / and offer
the barest acknowledgement / that this / is the end / we make it
outside to the crisp air / to the wide open space / to a night filled with
stars / only to realize that you left your phone behind /
in the crowd / we lose each other in the back track /
only to find each other again / by the double doors / when you
see me / there is something in the feathering crinkles at the corners of
your eyes / that makes me want to hold you / but the crush of people
/ is so present / it is only in the solitude of your truck / sitting beneath
the light /
that we can finally turn the corner / i say *it was as if everything i've
been feeling these last few months / was filling up that theater / as if
we were all feeling it together* / you agree / and you speak of the shoes
that were piled / in the halls of concentration camps / you visited in
germany / you say in a soft voice / and without the buffer of simile /
that each pair of shoes /
was a person / and your tears / are no different
from my own / and / our fears of that history / repeating / leave our
lips coated in salt / the risk of that violence reaching out to touch
more human beings / seems to buzz in the quiet of the engine /
america the brave / america the free / is bending at the waist / is
chained at the wrists / and i am anchoring myself to the faith / that
she will rise again / in kindness / redeemed / because the people will

not allow each other to fall / but / as we drive through the night / to the warmth of your home / the bells seem to toll in the distance
i do not close my eyes at the sound
i do not let go

of your hand.

some of this space

on the other side / of some distant port / i am still there / time
capsuled / in the act of falling / in love

your bed is a comfort / i do not know how to find / not even when i
am in it / how cliche: the world is ending /   around us /
a victim to our governance

and i still care that / my hand is on your shoulder / and the pad of
your thumb is running over my lip

how human: my fears / for i am struck by the not knowing if you are
feeling this too / this desire to speak to you / listen to you / be close
to you /

some instant replay of a past love's rejection / sends me tailspinning
into doubt / do you want this   hand to be your
comfort?

with each year that passes / i am more clearly defined / by my
capacity to love / i find myself

hoping you could want / to curl up and be safe / in some of this space

perhaps just one / of my ribs could be / carved with your name

perhaps the people i love / could be loved by you

i am / as ever / a hand reaching out in comfort / in hopes of offering
comfort

tonight / i sleep in your bed / and wake to place my hand on your
skin / there is a joy here that cannot overwhelm reality /
but there is joy

tonight we exist / in each others' arms

tomorrow you will sip coffee with me / in a room painted gold with sunlight / and it will be just one / of my interpretations of heaven

that is enough / to make me feel as though / perhaps / the world could end /

and people would fight / to come back to life again.

here

in memory of andrea gibson

the year milo turns ten
we finally fix the latches on the doors inside the house. for eight years
we fluttered from room to room with the doors wide open
milo and i and all the cats we've ever loved.

the year milo turns ten, fred, the ginger tabby who slept in my bed for
17 years, dies. i know i will love him when i'm 80.
i know he will walk up to me at those pearly gates and flop down on
his back. green eyes asking me to paint the carpet of heavenly grass
with his body. pet as a verb. pet on surround sound. when i die,
heaven will look so much like my own backyard that my heart will
break with the joy of it.
the year my son turns ten, andrea gibson dies. i imagine they were
right about all of it. even everything. even everything. perhaps when
you don't get enough time, you get to be a little more right.
all I know is that i lived long enough to find heaven in my back yard.
i lived, in part, due to a poet and a cat.
andrea, i hope you've met him, my fred. i hope you looked at each
other and he came over and butted his head against your leg to thank
you for each night your voice played on my stereo, hope on repeat,
while he held me in the warmth of his fur, his love. if you speak he
will know your voice.

i wrote the first draft of this poem wrapped in the arms of a sleeping
man who sees me as me even when i'm slumping into the darkness
while shitting myself on his toilet. vasovagal syncope taking hold.
taking me under. dylan's hands hold me up, abrade my skin. they say
stay.

you said stay. you said here is the only place left on the map. you said
write the poems. and i did, andrea, i did. but first i transcribed your
words onto my porch in sidewalk chalk. first i braided a rope to hold
myself here.
you said happiness would go extinct and come back. and it did,
andrea. it did.

this year, my son turned ten years old. the doors of our house latch now, but we leave them open—most of the time. the wallpaper on my desktop is a photo of milo's legs on top of mine, and my legs on top of dylan's. the moment before i took the picture i was so glad my couch

was too small. shortly before I took that photograph, i was laughing so hard my heart caught on fire.

andrea, my son turned ten years old this year and i was here to see it.

table setting

this table is full-to-bursting: books spread in disarray,
half-written songs crowd the corners, a cup of flowers:
picked as i walked the badlands—
a place where people say nothing grows—
and then there comes the food
and the wine
poured into wax-paper dixie cups.
this table is full-to-bursting
to think
last year

i stood in this same room
complaining of all the emptiness

With Thanks

Writing *the light can be something we love all on our own* allowed me to grow and change; to become the kind of person who could bear the weight of leaving the people I love when necessary, while simultaneously staying open to the right people. The ability to stop running and allow myself to heal and express and build a language of the self was not an easy skill to acquire. Making those difficult choices strengthened my understanding of what it means to be a good mother. It also allowed me to become the person I am today: a person who can love wholeheartedly and leave herself open to being supported by a caring partner. I look back on my past and feel so much gratitude to the child in me for making the choice to refuse to turn into someone cruel—despite the cruelty in the world around me at the time—and for making the decision to always tell the people I loved that I loved them, something that had never been offered to me at that point in my life. I am grateful for those past choices, for the child in me, for a little girl who chose to live because, against all evidence to the contrary, she believed that she would find a life of light, goodness, and joy—and she fought for it. My son, Milo, influenced so many of these poems. I am grateful everyday for his humor, kindness, and the curious way he observes the world. My partner, Dylan, came into my life at the end of the process of writing this collection. Everyday I feel so incredibly lucky that we found each other and so grateful for the work he has done over the course of his life to become the man I love—a man who takes the time to offer my son and me gentleness, play, support, and care. I am grateful to have found someone I am proud to share the rest of my life with, to grow together without end.

I have had far too many teachers to name here. If you have taught me, I am so grateful to you. To Dr. Annarose Steinke and Dr. Theodora Ziolkowski, who offered feedback and critique on these poems and others; and to Amy Graham, who listened: your support has helped me hear and trust my own voice. I consider there to be no greater gift that one person can give to another. My thanks goes beyond words.

Stephanie Glass lives in rural Nebraska with her son, Milo, and partner, Dylan Golden. Together with a constellation of loved ones, and a clowder of cats: Jelly Bean, Charlie, Fruit Loop, and Pants, they celebrate the joy that infuses the rhythm of their daily lives. Glass frequently disappears into the Nebraska Plains and Badlands for hiking and backpacking trips. In addition to nature, she draws inspiration for her poetry from literature, motherhood, queer identity, political activism, nature, post-traumatic growth following domestic violence, and the healing relationships she has built with those she loves. Her work has appeared in *Rattle Poetry Magazine, The Quarter(ly) Vol. XIII: This Is Where We Are Now, Writers in the Attic's Anthology: The Knot, the Moonstone Center for the Arts Anthology: Go Back to Where You Came From,* and The *Lavender Review.*

www.ingramcontent.com/pod-product-compliance
Lightning Source LLC
LaVergne TN
LVHW090539110826
845146LV00003B/1180